WHAT'S BENEATH

DRAWN

PEEKING UNDER
YOUR SKIN

by Karen Latchana Kenney

illustrated by Steven Wood

It is a hot summer day. Sweat rolls down your face. Your skin feels wet. Take a deep breath and fill your lungs with air.

Your body is a wonderful machine. Many systems work together so you can breathe, eat and play. But these systems are hidden. Your skin covers and protects them.

Want to see what your
body parts look like?
Turn the page to peek beneath ...

lung

lung

blood vessels

Your skin is just one thin layer of your body. Many body systems and parts lie beneath it. Each one has a special job.

Your body has many muscles, bones and organs. Can you spot the lungs? Lungs are one of many organs inside your body.

The maze of small lines are blood vessels. Blood vessels act like superhighways. They carry blood and oxygen throughout your body.

muscle

Cover up!

Let's start at the surface. The skin is a bumpy place. There are dips, pockets and hairs. The top layer is the epidermis. It sheds dead skin cells all the time.

Just below the epidermis is the thickest skin layer. It's called the dermis. See its fibres? They keep the skin strong. They also hold water. Many small blood vessels keep skin warm.

blood vessel

nerve

fibres

oil gland

epidermis

dermis

fat

DID YOU KNOW?

Two and a half square centimetres (1 square inch) is not very big. But in this space in your skin, you can find 6 metres (20 feet) of blood vessels, 100 oil glands and 1,000 nerve endings.

Next is the fat layer. It helps control your body's temperature. It also connects skin to your muscles and bones.

Keeping cool

If your body gets too hot, it won't work well. Sweat helps keep you cool.

Sweat comes from sweat glands. It is made mostly of water and salt. Sweat holds body heat. It travels through tiny tubes. Some tubes go directly to the skin's surface. Other tubes connect to hair follicles.

hair

hair follicle

sweat

sweat gland

DID YOU KNOW?

Sweat itself doesn't smell. Tiny creatures called bacteria make it stink. They live on skin. When sweat reaches the skin, bacteria change the sweat and make it smell.

When sweat dries, it takes heat away from the body. This process is like natural air-conditioning.

hair shaft

Hello, hair

Skin is covered in hair. The skin on top of your head usually has the most. Just below your scalp are close to 100,000 hair follicles. The follicles work non-stop to push hair through the skin. A single strand of hair begins at the hair root.

See the blood vessels? They feed the root's cells. The cells make a protein. The protein becomes the hair shaft. The hair grows longer and moves up the follicle.

gland

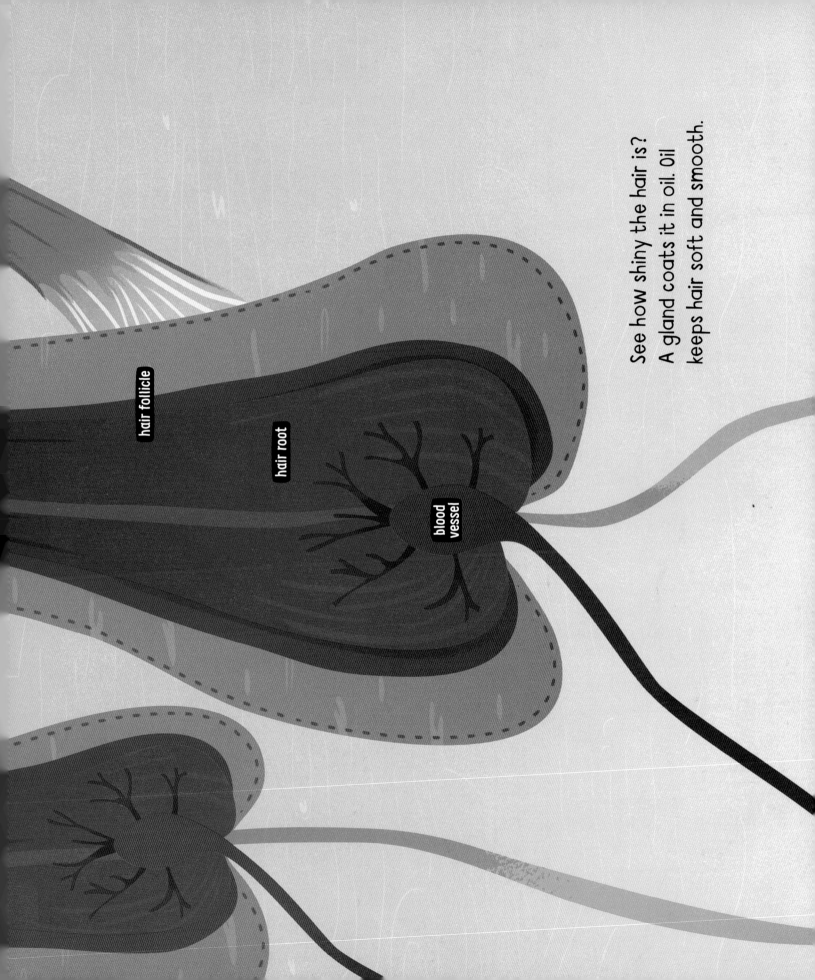

hair follicle

hair root

blood vessel

See how shiny the hair is? A gland coats it in oil. Oil keeps hair soft and smooth.

Superhighways

Your hair needs blood to grow. So does every other part of your body. Blood is made up of cells and plasma. It carries oxygen and nutrients throughout your body. Blood also takes away waste.

How does the blood move? It moves along "highways" of blood vessels. These highways are super-long. If placed in one line, your blood vessels would stretch 96,560 kilometres (60,000 miles)!

lung

lung

heart

artery

vein

capillary

plasma

blood cell

There are three kinds of blood vessels: veins, arteries and capillaries. Veins bring blood to the heart. The heart pumps oxygen from the lungs into the blood. Arteries move the oxygen-rich blood away from the heart. Capillaries branch off from arteries. They send the blood's oxygen to all the cells in your body. They also send carbon dioxide to the veins.

Breathing machine

Oxygen needs to get into your body to feed the blood. When you breathe in, air enters your nose or mouth. See where the air goes? It moves down the trachea.

See where the trachea splits? Those tubes are the bronchi. They lead to the lungs. The tubes get smaller and smaller. They become bronchioles.

oxygen

carbon dioxide

nose

mouth

Tiny sacs called alveoli fill with air. Capillaries surround each alveolus sac. The sac releases oxygen from the air into the capillaries. The capillaries also release carbon dioxide from the blood into the sac. Then you breathe out the carbon dioxide.

alveoli

capillaries

bronchioles

bronchi

lungs

trachea

Pumping blood

To move oxygen-rich blood throughout the body, you need a good pump. And you have one: your heart! This hardworking organ beats 100,000 times each day. It powers the body's circulatory system.

See how the heart has two sides? Each side sends out blood through the pulmonary artery. The blood travels to the lungs to pick up oxygen. From there it zips back to the heart through pulmonary veins. The oxygen-rich blood goes out to the body through the aorta. Each side of the heart has two chambers.

valve

valve

left atrium

left ventricle

right ventricle

aorta

right atrium

lung

valve

valve

pulmonary artery

pulmonary vein

lung

Valves act like doors. They open to let in blood to the chambers. The different valves and chambers keep the blood moving in the same direction.

The fuel factory

The body needs blood and oxygen to work well. It also needs fuel to power its systems. This fuel comes from food. Food gets broken down in the body's digestive system.

Let's follow a bite of apple. When you take a bite, your teeth break down the apple. Then the apple bits move down the oesophagus. Plop! They land in the stomach. A mixture of acids and enzymes in the stomach further breaks down the apple bits.

Muscles inside the stomach move the apple bits into a long tube called the small intestine. In the tube the bits break down even more.

Inside the small intestine, solid food changes into a liquid. Now the body absorbs the apple's nutrients into the blood.

oesophagus

stomach

large intestine

small intestine

Throw out the rubbish

Not all parts of food become fuel. The body has to get rid of liquids and solids. They leave the body as waste. The large intestine takes out solid waste.

It moves in waves. The waves push waste to the rectum. Waste collects there until it leaves the body through the anus.

large intestine

rectum

anus

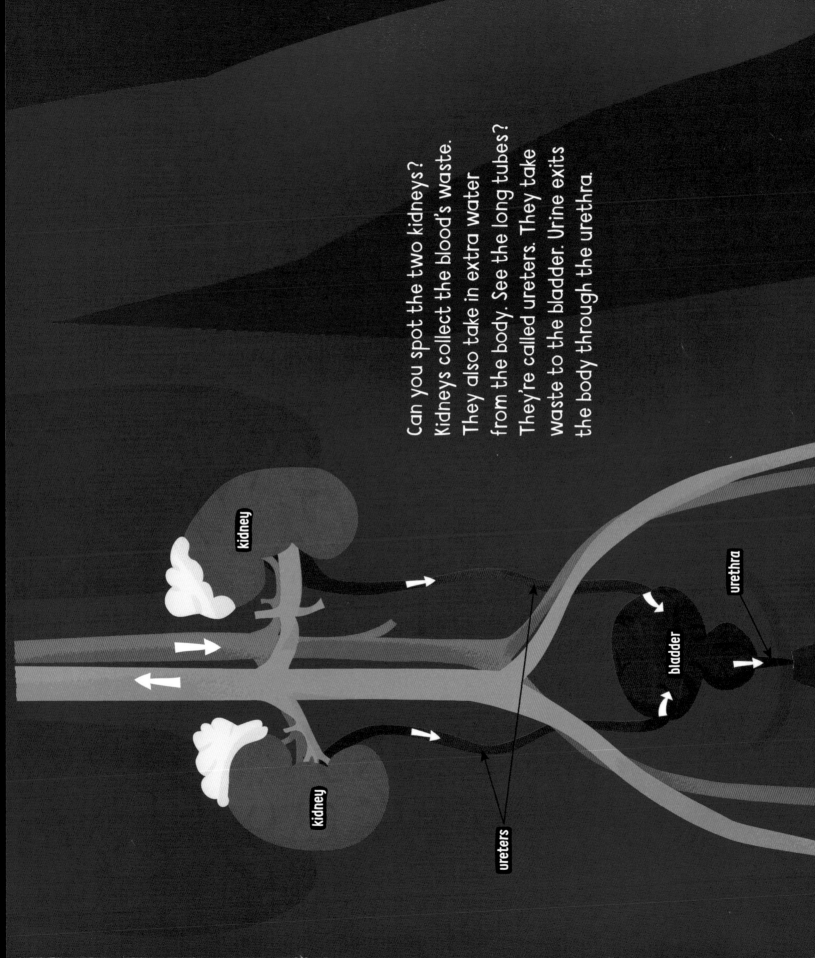

Can you spot the two kidneys? Kidneys collect the blood's waste. They also take in extra water from the body. See the long tubes? They're called ureters. They take waste to the bladder. Urine exits the body through the urethra.

kidney

kidney

ureters

bladder

urethra

Get the message?

You can sense when you have to go to the toilet. Your body sends your brain a message. Pain is another type of message. All messages travel through the body's nervous system. They travel faster than the blink of an eye.

Let's say you get stung by a bee. First the pain message moves through nerve fibres in the skin. The fibres connect to the spinal cord. Different nerve cells there receive and pass on the message. The nerve cells send the message to the brain.

The message reaches the thalamus. The thalamus knows which part of the brain needs the message. Parts of the brain control different movements and areas of the body. Your brain thinks of how to stop the stinging pain. It then sends a message back through the nervous system. It says, "Move your arm away from the bee!"

brain

thalamus

spinal cord

nerve fibres

DID YOU KNOW?
Nerves connect to your eyes, ears, mouth, skin and nose. The nerves send messages to your brain. That is how the brain sees, hears, tastes, touches and smells.

Taking control

Certain parts of the body need chemicals to work. These chemicals are the body's hormones.

See the different glands? They are hormone factories. They take materials from blood to make hormones. Then they release the hormones into the blood.

Look at the hypothalamus in the brain. Its hormones help you sleep and wake up. Hormones from the thyroid gland control how your body uses food. The thymus gland helps you fight off illness.

hypothalamus

pituitary gland

thyroid gland

Many parts of the body use hormones. They travel from glands to organs. They switch certain body functions on or off. Hormones control how you grow. They affect your moods. They control many other functions too.

adrenal gland

thymus gland

Bones and muscles

Hormones control how your skeleton grows. Your skeleton is your body's frame. It is made of the bones inside your body—more than 200! It holds you upright. It also protects organs inside the body. See where the bones come together and connect? Those places are called joints.

Many muscles cover your skeleton. See the tendon? It connects to the bone. Nerves send messages to muscles, telling them to move. The muscles stretch or shorten. Bones move with them.

The outside of a bone is hard and smooth. The layer below that is spongy. It has many holes. Some bones have red marrow. It makes blood cells. Other bones have yellow marrow. It is made up of fat cells.

Wipe the sweat from your skin. Find some shade. Time for a cold glass of lemonade! The human body is an amazing machine from the outside. And now you know how amazing it is inside too!

GLOSSARY

absorb soak up a liquid

acid liquid that can break down different materials, such as food

artery tube that carries blood from the heart to parts of the body

bacteria tiny living things that live on or around your body; some are helpful and some are harmful

carbon dioxide gas that people and animals breathe out

fibre long and thin thread of a material, such as a muscle

gland body organ that makes chemicals

muscle body part connected to bone that makes you move

nutrient protein, mineral or vitamin that makes you strong and healthy

organ body part that performs a certain job, such as the heart

oxygen gas found in air that people breathe in and use in their bodies

plasma liquid part of the blood

urine body's liquid waste

valve moving part that controls how a liquid or gas flows

vein tube that carries blood back to the heart

FIND OUT MORE
BOOKS

How to Build a Human Body, Tom Jackson (Scholastic, 2013)

My First Book of the Human Body, Jen Green (Collins, 2013)

Utterly Amazing Human Body, Robert Winston (DK, 2015)

WEBSITES

www.bbc.co.uk/bitesize/ks2/science/living_things/skeletons_muscles/read/1/

This site explains how bones and muscles work, with a game and a quiz to check your understanding.

www.ngkids.co.uk/science-and-nature/15-facts-about-the-human-body

Visit this site to find out amazing facts about the human body.

COMPREHENSION QUESTIONS

1. What do the kidneys do?

2. Look at the illustration of the lungs. Use it to explain what happens when you breathe in and out.

3. Describe how a sandwich gets from your mouth to your small intestine.

Raintree is an imprint of Capstone Global Library Limited, a company incorporated in England and Wales having its registered office at 264 Banbury Road, Oxford, OX2 7DY – Registered company number: 6695582

www.raintree.co.uk
myorders@raintree.co.uk

Text © Capstone Global Library Limited 2016
The moral rights of the proprietor have been asserted.

All rights reserved. No part of this publication may be reproduced in any form or by any means (including photocopying or storing it in any medium by electronic means and whether or not transiently or incidentally to some other use of this publication) without the written permission of the copyright owner, except in accordance with the provisions of the Copyright, Designs and Patents Act 1988 or under the terms of a licence issued by the Copyright Licensing Agency, Saffron House, 6–10 Kirby Street, London EC1N 8TS (www.cla.co.uk). Applications for the copyright owner's written permission should be addressed to the publisher.

ISBN 978 1 4747 1306 1 (hardback)
19 18 17 16 15
10 9 8 7 6 5 4 3 2 1

ISBN 978 1 4747 1310 8 (paperback)
20 19 18 17 16
10 9 8 7 6 5 4 3 2 1

British Library Cataloguing in Publication Data
A full catalogue record for this book is available from the British Library.

Editorial Credits
Jill Kalz, editor; Russell Griesmer, designer; Nathan Gassman, creative director; Katy LaVigne, production specialist

Acknowledgements
We would like to thank Marjorie Hogan, MD, Department of Pediatrics, Hennepin County (Minnesota) Medical Center, USA, for her invaluable help in the preparation of this book.

Every effort has been made to contact copyright holders of material reproduced in this book. Any omissions will be rectified in subsequent printings if notice is given to the publisher.

All the Internet addresses (URLs) given in this book were valid at the time of going to press. However, due to the dynamic nature of the Internet, some addresses may have changed, or sites may have changed or ceased to exist since publication. While the author and publisher regret any inconvenience this may cause readers, no responsibility for any such changes can be accepted by either the author or the publisher.

Printed and bound in China.

LOOK FOR ALL THE BOOKS IN THE SERIES:

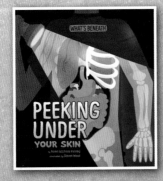